OLD
DUNST

A Collection of Photograph

Dunstable Priory, interior before 1945

The
Book
Castle

First published 1975

by White Crescent Press, Luton

This edition published
July 1989
by the Book Castle
12 Church Street, Dunstable, Bedfordshire

© The Book Castle
Printed by White Crescent Press Ltd., Luton.

ISBN 1 871199 05 0

*Front cover illustration: Town Hall, High Street North.
Built 1880, demolished 1964 (photo 1895).*

Back cover illustration: An early handbill.

Introduction to the 1989 edition

In the years since Bill Twaddle assembled this collection of old Dunstable pictures and wrote the Introduction, there have been a number of changes affecting the present-day town.

The modern shopping precincts have destroyed much of the character of the old town centre, but it is encouraging to note that more recently attempts have been made to preserve the best of what remains. Amongst the 'rescue' projects, may be mentioned:

the Anchor Archway in High Street North has been expertly refurbished by the Department of the Environment and the present owners of the building;

the new Eleanor Shopping precinct, with its modern bronze effigy of Queen Eleanor (wife of King Edward I) is a reminder of the fact that the town once boasted an Eleanor Cross at the cross-roads;

the façade of the High Street North Post Office building has been retained whilst the rest of the building has been demolished and replaced with modern offices;

the frontage of 20 High Street North has also been retained and some of the medieval wall-paintings found beneath the paper and distemper in the upstairs rooms have been mounted in the public area downstairs. Other wall-paintings from the same source are being mounted for display in the Dunstable Library;

26 Church Street (Mentmore House), a timber-framed building with jetty over the alley on the west side, has been saved from demolition;

Worthington George Smith's headstone and grave in the West Street Cemetery have been cleaned and put in good order;

and wall plaques have been fixed on buildings indicating the importance of certain sites in times past.

The formation of the Dunstable Museum Trust in 1980 and the modest display in the Dunstable Library have done much to awaken interest in our heritage and provide a focal point for this interest. More recently annual Heritage Weeks have served to focus attention on the richness of our heritage, particularly for the young.

Meanwhile, local government in the town has under-gone a number of changes. The nationwide local government re-organisation in 1974 abolished the Dunstable Borough Council. From then on Dunstable, together with Leighton/Linslade and all the villages around, became the responsibility of the South

Bedfordshire District Council. In 1985 Dunstable applied for and was granted Parish Council status (it chose to be known as a Town Council). This has meant that it can have its own precept to administer its parks, gardens, Cemetery, allotments, public conveniences, community centres and other local facilities. The Chairman of the Town Council holds the office of Town Mayor.

The population of the town has steadily increased to about 36,000. Much of this increase is due to the relatively good communications, making it a dormitory town for those working in London and the Greater London area north of the Thames.

Whereas Dunstable in the past was a place people tended to *pass through* on their way elsewhere, there is now much evidence that it is a place to which people *come*. And there is still much of interest both old and new to see when they arrive.

JOHN LUNN

Introduction to the 1975 edition

Dunstable's High Street follows the alignment of the ancient Watling Street from London to the North and the North East. The even more ancient Icknield Way from East Anglia to the South West crossed the Watling Street near to the town For the last 850 years the route has followed Church Street and West Street on to the Downs

So much has happened in Dunstable since the Romans marched north to the most northerly defences of their vast empire. The town has been rebuilt many times. Once it was a compact mediaeval market town gradually extending along the four main roads with a great Priory and two monasteries and a population of a few hundreds. From a modest area of 453 acres, the extensions of the boundaries came with the establishment of a printing works and the opening of two engineering works which changed the character of Dunstable to that of an industrial town.

The year 1933 brought the last extension of the Borough boundaries and the arrival of two great motor manufacturing companies led to the steady increase in population from approximately 5,000 in 1900 to the present 30,000.

Here is a collection of photographs covering rather less than 100 years of the town's history. There seems to be no limit to the number of old photographs but unfortunately many are unsuitable for reproduction and in many cases they are not dated.

Many aspects of the town are recorded. Ashton Grammar School (or Dunstable School as it was called) is well chronicled. Carnivals, processions and fête days are included as important events.

The dating of the photographs has proved to be a most formidable part of the task. In some cases the only guide to the period has been the names on shop fronts, or the position and design of a telegraph post. The publishers will welcome any suggestions for future editions.

Many people have made contributions towards this collection of old photographs and we record our thanks to: Bedfordshire Record Office, Dunstable Borough Gazette, Luton Museum & Art Gallery, Mr F. Hackett and Mr Richard Hagen, Dunstable Library, Miss Bertha M. Eyre, Mrs Vera Day, Miss D. Lester, Miss G. Lester, Miss E. Costin, Mrs E. Wilson, Mr T. W. Bagshawe (and for access to the Bagshawe Collection), Mr C. E. Bourne, Mr F. W. Clarke, Mr J. Dandy, Mr James Dyer, Mr B. G. England, Mr C. G. Grinonneau, Mr E. C. Hawes, Mr H. Joyce, Mr W. T. Lack, Mr K. A. Larking, Mr N. Newson, Mr R. Norris, Mr B. J. Scott, Mr C. D. Smith, Mr R. W. S. Smith, Mr P. Staines, Mr L. G. Tearle, Mr H. Weeks, Mr C. Wilson, Mr I. Williams.

W. TWADDLE

'When we build, let us think that we build for ever. Let it not be for the present delight, nor for present use alone, let it be such work as our descendants will thank us for, and let us think, as we lay stone on stone, that a time is to come when these stones will be held sacred because our hands have touched them and that men will say as they look upon the labour and wrought substance of them, "See! this our fathers did for us".'

RUSKIN – *The Seven Lamps of Architecture*

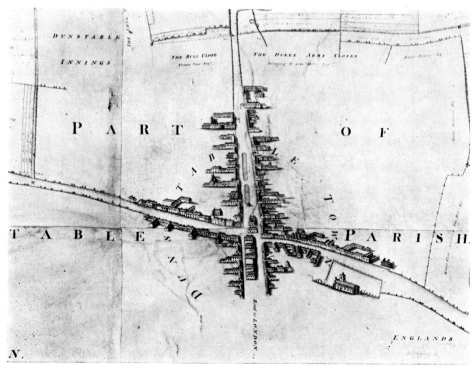

A Map of Dunstable, drawn by T. Richardson in 1766. Note the two horse ponds

6

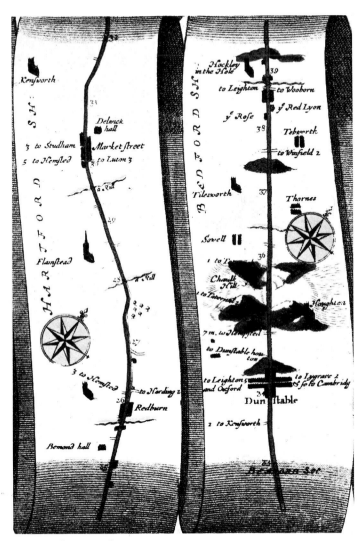

John Ogilby's Road Map, 1675

Passage between Ashton and   *Passage in Church Street*
High Street   *'Little Alley'*

Old passages at Dunstable, 1887
Drawn by Worthington G. Smith

Passage from High Street to   Passage between Ashton and
Church 'Church Alley'   High Street

Old passages at Dunstable, 1887
Drawn by Worthington G. Smith

9

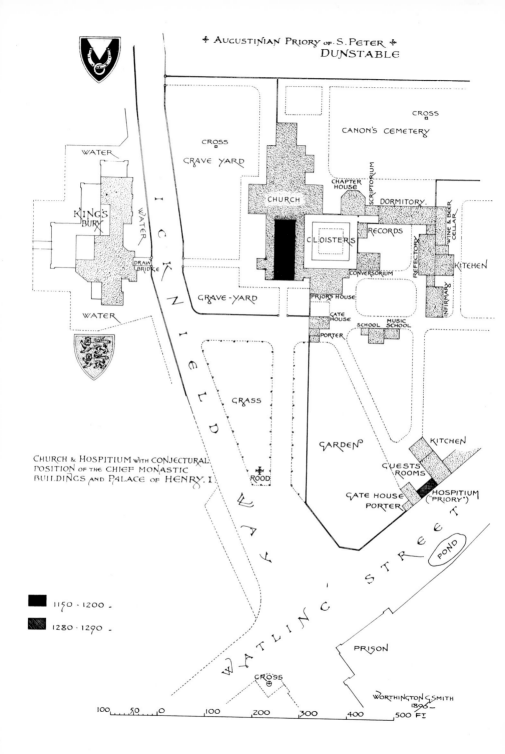

✠ AUGUSTINIAN PRIORY of S. PETER ✠
DUNSTABLE

CROSS

CANON'S CEMETERY

CROSS

GRAVE YARD

CHAPTER HOUSE

SCRIPTORIUM

DORMITORY

CHURCH

CLOISTERS

RECORDS

WINE & BEER CELLAR

WATER

KINGS BURY

WATER

DRAW BRIDGE

CONVERSORIUM

REFECTORY

KITCHEN

WATER

GRAVE-YARD

PRIORS HOUSE

INFIRMARY

GATE HOUSE

SCHOOL SCHOOL

MUSIC

PORTER

GRASS

GARDEN

KITCHEN

CHURCH & HOSPITIUM with CONJECTURAL
POSITION of the CHIEF MONASTIC
BUILDINGS and PALACE of HENRY I

ROOD

GUESTS ROOMS

GATE HOUSE
PORTER

HOSPITIUM
("PRIORY")

POND

WATLING STREET

1150 - 1200 -

1280 - 1290 -

PRISON

CROSS

WORTHINGTON G. SMITH
1896 -

100   50   0   100   200   300   400   500 FT

IO

ARMS OF DUNSTABLE.

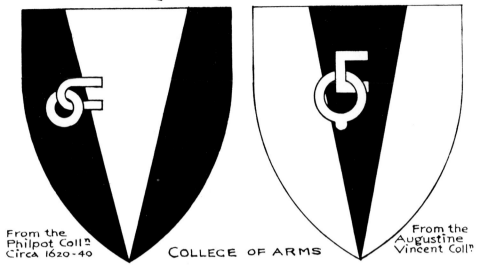

From the
Philpot Colln
Circa 1620-40

COLLEGE OF ARMS

From the
Augustine
Vincent Colln

Date of Shield from Henry III to end of 14th Centy.

Sable a Pile argent
thereon a Staple and
Ring argent

Argent a Pile sable
thereon a Staple and
Ring argent

Date of Shield, after 14 Centy to modern times

From Tanner's Notitia Monastica
1737

From Dugdale's Monasticon
1830

Field (background) varying
sable (black) and gules (red)
Pile varying argent (silver)

WORTHINGTON G SMITH - 1906

II

Drawing of the corner of West Street and High Street by Worthington G. Smith. 'Market day, Dunstable, early morning', 1895

Crossroads showing West Street prior to 1900. Limbrey, tinsmith, coppersmith and ironmonger was established here before 1843

High Street South (west side) and West Street, circa 1890

High Street North showing Grove House on left. Built as 'The Duke's Arms' mid-eighteenth century, one time home of the Bagshawe family, now municipal offices, 1909

High Street North, looking south, circa 1890

Middle Row, looking north, showing original painted telegraph posts erected 1863, circa 1890

14

High Street North showing the 'Red Lion', circa 1900

High Street North showing old Post Office, circa 1900

15

Church Street, looking east, circa 1906

Church Street scene, circa 1910

'The Grey House', 59 High Street South, eighteenth century 'Star' Inn, nineteenth century straw hat and bonnet manufacturing. Photograph taken about 1870 showing employees

Town Hall, High Street North, purchased by Corporation 1866. Clock Tower erected 1869, destroyed by fire 1879 (circa 1870)

Dunstable branch of the British Legion annual remembrance parade and service, 11 July 1938

Chalk Hill, showing road to Sewell on the left and the Watling Street in foreground, circa 1910

18

Frances Ashton Almshouses, corner of West Street and Ashton Street, now demolished and replaced by new houses in Bull Pond Lane. From a drawing by Thomas Fisher about 1815. Note stocks and whipping post in foreground

Blandina Marshe, Church Street 'Ladies' Lodge'. Built 1743. From a drawing by Thomas Fisher about 1815

I. J. & G. Cooper's hat factory (previously Burr's Brewery). High Street North site present Post Office (1859)

Priory House and Munt & Brown hat factory, 1859 (factory has been demolished)

The 'White Horse' Inn. Church Street, 1950. Tudor with decorated oak beams, eighteenth century front. Now demolished

Remains of the Royal Palace at Dunstable from an engraving dated 1816. Now Kingsbury Court, 'Old Palace Lodge' and the 'Norman King'

Tollgate south of Dunstable, built soon after 1723, opposite Turnpike Farm. Later re-built first at Kensworth Lynch (about 1835) then finally close to 'Half Moon' public house. The turnpike Trust controlled the road from St Albans to 'The Black Bull' in Dunstable

A visit of the Lord Mayor of London to 'The Old Sugar Loaf'. Said to be Sir Thomas Vansittart Bowater, 1914

Frederick Freeman of Kingsbury House in front of the 'Red Lion', driving his four-in-hand from London to Coventry, 1904

'Old Sugar Loaf' Hotel bus in Matthew Street, circa 1900

Kingsbury Stables, now part of 'The Norman King'

Chew's School, High Street South. Built and endowed 1715 by Frances Ashton, Jane Cart (sisters of William Chew) and Thomas Aynscombe (nephew) to accommodate forty boys

Ashton Grammar School, High Street North, opened 1888

Dunstable School Cadet Corps Band. Jubilee Parade outside Municipal offices, 19 June 1938

Worthington George Smith's house, 'Hawthorn Cottage', 121 High Street South, (later re-numbered 142). Demolished 1959

'Prosperous Row' 1970 (now demolished)

'The Foresters Arms', nineteenth century. Demolished 1973

'Old Anchor' Inn gateway, late sixteenth century

The 'Red Lion' yard showing part of previous inn, 1930. Now demolished

Dog Kennel Walk, 1906. Ancient footpath to Houghton Regis

'Ye Olde Retreat' for many years Rixson's antique showrooms, 43 High Street South. Now demolished

Looking south. 'The Tower House' on left, Bennetts Brewery on right (1907), both demolished

Coronation of King George V, Mr R. P. Graham conducts a choir of local schoolchildren.
22 June 1911

Peace Celebration Parade, 1919

Annual Sunday School procession from Wesleyan Methodist Chapel in High Street North circa 1905

Ashton C of E Boys' and Girls' School as it was in 1933. Built in 1865

Norman Arch West Front Dunstable Priory from a drawing by Worthington G. Smith circa 1885

Restoration of Guest Hall (Priory House) drawn by Worthington G. Smith

Wesleyan Church, The Square. Built 1845 destroyed by fire 1908

Bagshawe & Co Ltd started in London about 1880, moved to Dunstable 1906. Thomas Tilling Ltd acquired controlling interest in 1953, closed down 1972

Wesleyan Methodist Church, The Square, Foundation stone laying ceremony, 31 May 190

J. Harrison Carter Ltd (Engineers, Bull Pond Lane) work force 1906. (Founded 1894, now demolished)

The Rev Canon W. W. C. Baker, MA (Rector of Dunstable 1903–24) with church officials and church workers, 1924

'Borough Band' or 'Franklin's Band', 1905

The 'Excelsior' Silver Prize Band, 1902

Dunstable Town Football Club, 1912–13

Cross & Co Ltd (High Street South), mixed hockey team, 1919

An outing with Mr George E. Costin of West Street driving his 'four-in-hand'. Prior to 191

High Street North, cycle and motor-cycle repairer

30th Beds (1st Dunstable) Troop of Boy Scouts. Winners of Roffe Flag (County Champion-ship), 1919

Dunstable School Cadet Corps drum and bugle band (formed 1919) en route to Reading for annual parade in aid of Royal Berkshire Hospital, 15 May 1938

C Company 6th Bedfordshire Battalion Home Guard, 1944

Dunstable Voluntary Fire Brigade, 1901
Back row: Fred Dyer, Ernest White, Ernest Eustace. Front row: Henry Turner, Albert Owen,
George Baldock and Ernest Mooring

Corporation road repairers in West Street, 1922

Party from 'The Globe Inn', Winfield Street. Seated in centre behind front row Councillor G. 'Dobbin' Holt. 1933

Chain-makers, Bagshawe & Co Ltd. Seated front left: Mr Bill Hickinbottom, foundry foreman, circa 1920

Wesleyan Methodist Church trustees with minister Rev J. W. Millward, 1909

Wesleyan Methodist Church trustees with minister Rev A. E. Follows, 1950

Operatic Society. Cast for 'Tom Jones', 1927

Adult School, circa 1920

Hawthorn Tennis Club, 1912

Dunstable School, Preparatory School 1935, Forms 1 and 2 outside Ashton Lodge with Mr C. L. Harris

Motor Cycling Club, annual dinner at 'The Old Sugar Loaf', 1930

Dunstable School, Boarder Reunion Dinner in 'The Old Sugar Loaf', 18 March 1939

Dunstable School Staff, Jubilee year 1938. Left to right back row: F. R. Speke, F. M. Bancroft, R. Poirier, A. C. Wadsworth, W. H. Brock, F. Cadle. Front row: C. L. Harris, L. A. Boskett, W. D. Coales, A. F. R. Evans (headmaster), H. J. Butters, C. P. Le Huray and W. T. La

Prime Minister of Pakistan, K. W. Nazimuddin visits his school dormitory, headmaster G. F. Bailey on extreme left, 1952

Dunstable Repertory Company. Cast of 'This Happy Breed', 1948

Dunstable Repertory Company. Cast of 'Quiet Weekend', 1949

Dunstable Girls' Choir, 1955. Winners of twenty-three awards

Dunstable Girls' Choir, 1955, group of soloists

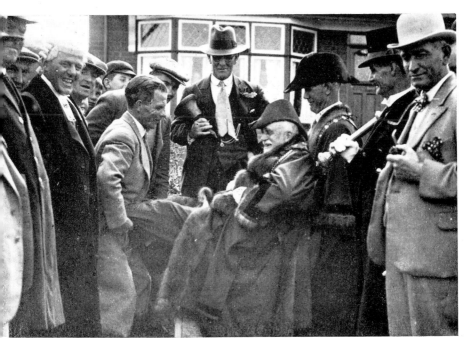

Extension of Borough boundaries 1 April 1933 to 2,035 acres, population 9,932; 2,925 houses. The Mayor of Luton, Councillor G. Wistow Walker being 'bumped' on the new boundary stone by the Mayor of Dunstable Alderman Alfred Cook and Councillor Horace J. Darby

Bagshawe Bowls Club, 1958

Motor car accident, Watling Street. Said to be the first fatal motor car accident on the A5, 190

Daimler car driven by Mr G. A. Grinoneau about 1905

Road Motors Ltd bus service to Luton, 1919

Traffic on the Icknield Way – the horseman Mr J. Christmas Willimot was the last ostler at 'The Old Sugar Loaf', circa 1920

High Street North, elephants and camels on their way from the railway station to Whipsnade prior to the opening of the Zoo, 1931

High Street, Houghton Regis.

irca 1895

ottages at Totternhoe (now demolished), 1895

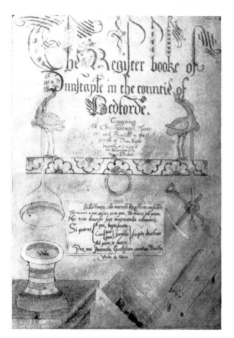

Parish Church Register, illustrated by John Willis, 1600

Worthington George Smith, FLS, FRAI, FRSA(IRELAND), HON FR HORTS (1833–1917)
Architectural draughtsman, botanist, archaeologist, historian, author and book illustrator.
First Freeman of the Borough of Dunstable, 1903

James Waterlow 1790–1876, founder of Waterlow & Sons Ltd

Archaeological find on the Friary site. Mediaeval Bee-hive oven (photo c.1965)

AC Delco, sparking plug assembly. Founded as Sphinx Mfg Co, Birmingham 1898, amalgamated with AC Spark Plug, Michigan, 1923, acquired by General Motors Ltd, 1927. Moved to Dunstable 1934

Bagshawe & Co Ltd, elevator, about 1913

Bagshawe & Co Ltd, modern conveyor system, 1963

An early handbill

'The Rifleman' or 'Rifle Volunteer' at the foot of the Downs, circa 1908

R. B. Tompkins, boot and shoe makers shop, 5 High Street South, 1903

Mr Walter Baker outside his ironmonger's shop, 14 Church Street in 1903. The shop closed down when Church Street was developed in 1964

The Old Mill, West Street. Built in 1839. It is 60ft high, five floors, and the walls at the base a 3ft 6in thick, circa 1909

Fire Brigade's demonstration, 1911

INDEX

Books Published by
THE BOOK CASTLE

JOURNEYS INTO BEDFORDSHIRE: Anthony Mackay
Foreword by The Marquess of Tavistock
A lavish book of over 150 evocative ink drawings.

. . .

LOCAL WALKS: SOUTH BEDFORDSHIRE and NORTH CHILTERNS:
Vaughan Basham
Twenty seven thematic circular walks.

. . .

JOHN BUNYAN: HIS LIFE and TIMES: Vivienne Evans
Foreword by the Bishop of Bedford
Bedfordshire's most famous son set in his seventeenth century context.

. . .

DUNSTABLE IN DETAIL: Nigel Benson
A hundred of the town's buildings and features, past and present, plus town-trail map.

. . .

ROYAL HOUGHTON: Pat Lovering
Illustrated history of Houghton Regis from earliest times to the present day.

. . .

OLD HOUGHTON, INCLUDING UPPER HOUGHTON, NOW PART OF DUNSTABLE: Pat Lovering
Over 170 photographs of Houghton Regis during the last 100 years.

. . .

A LASTING IMPRESSION: Michael Dundrow
An East End boy's wartime experiences as an evacuee on a Chilterns farm at Totternhoe.

. . .

ECHOES: TALES AND LEGENDS OF BEDFORDSHIRE AND HERTFORDSHIRE: Vic Lea
Thirty, compulsively retold historical incidents.

Further titles are in preparation.

All the above are available via any bookshop,
or from the publisher and bookseller
THE BOOK CASTLE,
12 Church Street, Dunstable, Bedfordshire LU5 4RU. Tel (0582) 605670